It's Cool To...
Give to Charity

The Confident Ummah

Copyright © 2022

All rights reserved. Without limiting rights under the copyright reserved above, no part of this publication may be reproduced, stored, introduced into a retrieval system, distributed or transmitted in any form or by any means, including without limitation photocopying, recording, or other electronic or mechanical methods, without the prior written permission of the publisher, except in the case of brief quotations embodied in critical reviews and certain other non-commercial uses permitted by copyright law.

The scanning, uploading, and/or distribution of this document via the internet or via any other means without the permission of the publisher is illegal and is punishable by law. Please purchase only authorized editions and do not participate in or encourage electronic piracy of copyrightable materials

About the Author

Welcome to The Confident Ummah, Adab Series. We were inspired to create books for our children and ummah so they can refer to them throughout their early years and better themselves as Muslims.

The first 10 years of a child's life are the most impressionable. This is when their foundations are formed and so it is the best time to encourage positive traits, so they are equipped with the tools to live healthy and balanced lives through which they worship and serve Allah ﷻ.

Each storybook has been designed to focus on a main principle, followed by related Qur'an/Hadith quotes. The moral of the story section highlights the core lessons from the storybook. Finally, we have included an activity page which is designed to encourage your child to implement the story's lessons.

Our stories are based on questions our children ask us and scenarios we have come across in our daily lives whilst homeschooling them.

We ask Allah ﷻ to accept our efforts in spreading useful knowledge and to strengthen (and unite) our ummah. Ameen.

Bismillahir Rahmanir Raheem

In the name of Allah, the Most Beneficent, the Most Merciful

Abdullah and Taiba were walking past the shops when they saw a car and paint set that they wanted.
"Daddy, can you buy these for us, please?" They ask nicely.
"But you already own toys like these," replies their father.
"Yes, but these are shiny and new," they both said.

"My children, we must be grateful for what we already own," says their father.
"Does that mean your not going to buy it for us then?" Asks Taiba.
"No my darling. We must earn these things. I want to teach you something first," says their father.

The next day they visited a charity in East London. "Why are we here daddy and what are all these posters on the wall?" Asks Adbullah. Just then, a worker comes to greet them.

"Assalam aulaikum children. Welcome to our charity. My name is uncle Hamza."
"Waalaikum assalam uncle. Who are all these people in the posters?" Asks Abdullah.

Assalam aulaikum - peace be upon you
Waalaikum assalam - and upon you too

"They are the families and people that we help.
"But his house only has one room," says Abdullah.
"That is correct," replies uncle Humza.

"Do they have toys?" Asks Abdullah.
"Only a few that get donated. Any money the family are able to make goes towards food and basic items," replies uncle Humza.

8

"Can we do something to help them?" Abdullah asks.
"That is a great question and the answer is yes! You can help raise money for them and can provide them with food, water and a fixed home insha'Allah," says uncle Humza.

Insha'Allah - If God wills

"Daddy, quickly give uncle all the money you have in your pocket. We need to help these families right now!"
Taiba says quickly.

"My sweet Taiba, if we fundraise, we can gather a larger amount of money to send over. How does that sound?" Says her father.
"I love that idea, how do we start?" Asks Taiba.
"I will show you," replies her father.

On the following Saturday, they went to a local market. A stall was selling some goods.
"Can I purchase all of those items please?" Asks the father.

"What are we going to do with all this food?" Asks Taiba.
"We are going to package it up nicely and sell it to people to collect donations for the charity we visited, insha'Allah," he replies.

Insha'Allah - If Good wills

Back home, their mother buys some nice looking boxes and ribbon to present the food nicely. Everyone stands in a line putting the food into each box. Even Little baby Zaynab tried to help.

The next day, they went door-to-door knocking.
"What do I say when someone opens the door?" Asks Abdullah.
"Good question son. Say your name and tell them what you are selling and why. I will be with you. We will do it together."

Abdullah knocks on the first door.
"Hello, my name is Abdullah. We are selling boxes of cookies for £5. The money will go to charity. Are you interested?"
"How yummy! Yes please! What a great job you children are doing!" The man says.

After knocking on many doors, Adbullah and Taiba learnt to speak with different people and this increased their confidence. Some people were nice, some were generous and some were rude but it didn't matter because they were having fun!

They returned to the charity the following week and Abdullah handed over the money they had made. "Masha'Allah, you made all this money? You should be very proud! I hope you know you are able to make a big difference with this money!" Said uncle Hamza.

"We really enjoyed ourselves and I love knowing it's going to help others," says Abdullah. Uncle Humza rewarded them with medals and stickers for their hard work. "May Allah accept your efforts in easing the difficulties for others, Ameen," uncle Humza says.

Back at home, Abdullah and Taiba run to greet their father by the front door.
"Assalam aulaikum my children! I have bought you the paint set and toy car. You have earned these for your hard work. I am very proud of you both!" They give their father a big hug.

Moral of the Story

1) In this story we encourage our children to support charitable causes proactively and on a consistent basis. We also teach respect by referring to the charity worker as 'uncle' instead of using his first name.

2) We want to teach that regardless of age, you can always take part and support in some way - even if it is just holding the collection bucket.

3) It is also good practice to teach children to give away belongings of value so they can maintain a healthy distance from worldly items instead of becoming consumed and enslaved by them in adulthood. It is crucial for money to not enter our hearts.

4) Only seeking the pleasure and assistance of Allah ﷻ is a core lesson to teach. In our opinion, if you raise a child to rely solely on Allah ﷻ throughout life, you would have done a good job.

5) We also teach that raising money and doing good deeds is associated with positive feelings and improving self-confidence. Achievement and competency also build inner confidence.

6) Charitable work also teaches communication skills and how to relate to different personality types.

The Prophet ﷺ said the following in relation to charity:
"Sadaqah (charity) extinguishes sin as water extinguishes fire" [Hadith, Tirmidhi].
"Charity does not reduce wealth." [Hadith, Muslim].

Activity

1) Start by discussing what charity means to you and the different ways you can contribute. Look at the different projects and choose one that you feel passionate about. Decide whether you will donate your money or your time towards supporting this cause.

2) When we fundraise, we ensure that not only do our children raise the funds themselves but also hand the raised profits over to the charities. This will train their minds to (a) remain detached from money, and (b) realise that their hard work has benefitted others who are less fortunate.

3) Find a donation box and give your children change to put in them. In most occasions, people are holding the boxes and calling for people to donate.

4) Buy some food for a homeless person and get your children to hand it over.

Always remember - charitable acts are all part of a long-term goal and something that is constantly a part of your life.
It's a marathon and not a sprint, so always pace yourself.